你好

Nǐ Hǎo

③

Odelle Chen

Student Workbook
Intermediate Level

by

Shumang Fredlein ● Paul Fredlein

ChinaSoft

Nǐ Hǎo 3 – Student Workbook – Intermediate Level

First published 1995; reprinted 1997, 1998, 2000

New edition 2003; reprinted 2005, 2007, 2008

ChinaSoft Pty Ltd   ABN : 61 083 458 459

P.O. Box 845, Toowong, Brisbane, Qld 4066, AUSTRALIA

Telephone   (61-7) 3371 - 7436

Facsimile   (61-7) 3371 - 6711

www.chinasoft.com.au

Written by Shumang Fredlein（林淑满）& Paul Fredlein

Illustrated by Zhengdong Su（苏正东）& Xiaolin Xue（薛晓林）

Edited by Sitong Jan（詹絲桐）

Typeset by ChinaSoft on Apple Macintosh

Printed in Australia by Watson Ferguson & Company, Brisbane

Textbook, audio cassettes/CDs and Games software also available.

ISBN 1 876739 19 3

Foreword

The *Ni Hao 3 Student Workbook* is a learning activity book based on the content introduced in the *Ni Hao 3 Textbook – Chinese Language Course, Intermediate Level*. This workbook contains a variety of activities that provide opportunities for students to practise the four communication skills – listening, speaking, reading and writing. Activities can be adapted to suit students' needs and abilities, e.g. the listening exercises can be used for speaking; the reading and writing exercises can be used for both listening and speaking.

The listening exercises for each lesson are included in the Teacher's Handbook and on audio cassettes/CDs. The teacher may play the cassette/CD to the class, or alternatively, read out the passages from the Teacher's Handbook. Answers to all the questions in this book are included in the Teacher's Handbook.

Chinese characters are used in conjunction with Pinyin to reinforce reading and writing skills. Students are not required to write exclusively in characters, but are encouraged to use a combination of Pinyin and characters. The Textbook lists characters students should learn to write. These characters are also included in the *Writing Exercise* section of this book. Students should always write characters in the correct stroke order and in good proportion. By doing this, it provides the foundation for beautiful handwriting which is always appreciated by Chinese.

Contents

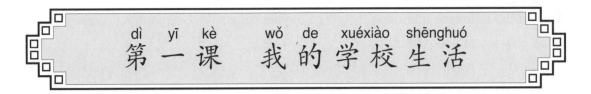

A Imagine this is your school timetable. Tell your Chinese friends about your classes.

	Monday	Tuesday	Wednesday	Thursday	Friday
1	maths	science	English	Chinese	history
2	maths	geography	science	Chinese	English
3	history	music	maths	history	English
4	English	music	Chinese	geography	science
5	Chinese	maths	geography	art	maths
6	physical ed.	Chinese	history	science	home economics
7	physical ed.	English	art	science	home economics

Answer the following questions:

1. 你星期一有什么课？

我星期一有数学,历史、

2. 你星期二第四节是什么课？

我星期二第四节是音乐课

3. 你星期三有没有汉语课？

_____

4. 你星期四有几节数学课？

_____

5. 你星期五上午有英语课吗？

_____

B Answer the following questions according to your timetable. Use complete sentences with as many characters as possible.

1. 你今天下午有什么课？

_____

2. 你明天上午有什么课？

_____

3. 你星期四有什么课？

_____

4. 你上一节是什么课？

_____

5. 你下一节是什么课？

_____

6. 你星期四第五节是什么课？

_____

7. 你星期二第六节是什么课？

_____

8. 你昨天最后一节是什么课？

_____

C Imagine you have a pen friend in China. Write your school timetable in Chinese and explain to him/her your likes and dislikes concerning each subject.

Your school timetable:

课程表　　　　　姓名：　　　　　　班级：					
period＼day					

Write what you like or dislike about some of your subjects.

_____

_____

_____

_____

D Use complete sentences to answer the following questions according to the information given.

Michael　　　小英　　　Jason　　　Michelle　　　Arnold　　　Kylie

1. Michael 数学考得怎么样？

_____

2. 小英历史考得怎么样？

_____

3. Jason 科学考试得了多少分？

_____

4. Michelle 的英语考得很好吗？

_____

5. Arnold 昨天的历史考试考得还不错，是吗？

_____

6. Kylie 的地理考得怎么样？她考了多少分？

_____

E Choose an appropriate word for each sentence, then use that word to write a sentence of your own.

jiè	huán		jìde	yídìng	rúguǒ	bié
借	还	忘	记得	一定	如果	别

1. 你的红笔 _____ 我，可以吗？

_____

2. 你明天的游泳课，别 _____ 了带游泳衣。
（bié）

_____

3. 我弟弟昨天借你的钱，你什么时候 _____ ？
（jiè）

_____

4. 拿去用吧！可是 _____ 要记得还我。
（ná）　　　　　　　　（jìde）

_____

F Rewrite the following sentences in Chinese using 如果……的话

1. I will return the money to you tomorrow, if I remember.

_____

2. She will come on Monday, if it doesn't rain.

_____

3. We can go to the movies together, if you are free.

_____

G Listen to the conversation between 黄小兰 Huáng Xiǎolán and her mother; then answer the following questions.

1. Where is 黄小兰 Huáng Xiǎolán going?

2. What did 黄小兰 Huáng Xiǎolán's mother remind her to do and why?

3. Did 黄小兰 Huáng Xiǎolán take her mother's advice? Why or why not?

4. What lesson does 黄小兰 Huáng Xiǎolán have this afternoon and what is the activity?

In the box below, paste the copy of the conversation given to you by your teacher to further check your understanding. Use this copy to hold a conversation with your partner.

H Answer the following questions according to the illustration. Use complete sentences with as many characters as possible.

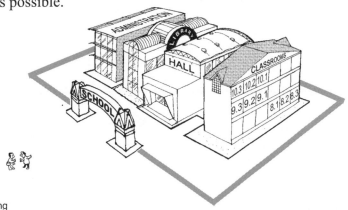

　　　　dòng　xíngzhèng
1. 哪一栋是行政楼？

_____

　　lǐtáng
2. 礼堂在哪里？

_____

　　túshūguǎn
3. 图书馆在哪里？

_____

4. 八年级三班的教室在几楼？

_____

5. 九年级二班的教室在几楼？

_____

6. 十年级二班的教室在三楼什么地方？

_____

7. 哪一间是九年级一班的教室？

_____

八

I Imagine you have a new classmate. Draw a school map and describe to her the relative positions of major buildings and the location of your classroom.

Your map:

Your description:

_____

_____

_____

_____

_____

J Interview students who were not born in Australia and find out: 1. if they are Australian, 2. how long they have been in Australia, 3. how long they have been learning English, 4. how long they have been learning Chinese.

The questions you need for the interview:

1. _____

2. _____

3. _____

4. _____

Fill in the information you obtain and report the results of your interview to your class.

Names				

Your findings: 1. Percentage of students who are Australian citizens.

2. Average length of time living in Australia.

3. Percentage of students who learnt English before coming to Australia.

4. Average length of time learning Chinese.

K Rewrite the following in Chinese, using as many characters as possible.

+

1. What does ' 为什么 ' mean?

_____

2. How do you write 'wèishénme' in Chinese?

_____

3. Sorry! what did you say?

_____

4. Sorry! I didn't hear it clearly.

_____

5. How do you say 'why' in Chinese?

_____

6. Do you understand it?

_____

7. Do you have any questions?

_____

8. Have you done your homework?

_____

L Rearrange the characters in each question to make a sentence/conversation.

1. 今下什午有你么天课？我午有美和地术下理。

_____

2. 你天学有数课吗明？有我没。

_____

3. 她天的历不史考考昨得还试错。

_____

4. 九室四在班的教哪年儿？在楼学三教楼。

_____

5. 们的我教室边在右一间最后。

_____

6. 英们是我同班的新小学。

_____

7. 你习汉多语久学了？学两了了年半我。

_____

8. 我弟昨了忘做作弟天业。

_____

M What would you say to your Chinese friend in the following situations? Use complete sentences with as many characters as possible.

1. You want to borrow a pen from him.

_____

2. You want him to remember to return the money to you tomorrow.

_____

3. You tell him it is too hot out here and suggest going inside.

_____

4. You would like to know which floor his classroom is on.

_____

5. You tell him that your classroom is on the second floor, the second room on the left.

_____

6. You would like to know how long he has been in Australia.

_____

7. You would like to know how long he has been learning English.

_____

8. You would like to know whether he has done his chemistry homework.

_____

N Imagine you are 李秋 Lǐ Qiū and write in your diary about your new friends and your first day at your new school. Use as many characters as possible.

十
四

O Combine the characters in the box to make as many words or expressions as you can.

上	学	班	美	级	校	英	一	语	汉	科	数	作	教	地	师	来
室	年	去	历	第	起	术	进	课	出	拿	考	试	业	史	本	理

words/expressions   meaning   words/expressions   meaning

_____ : _____   _____ : _____

_____ : _____   _____ : _____

_____ : _____   _____ : _____

_____ : _____   _____ : _____

_____ : _____   _____ : _____

_____ : _____   _____ : _____

_____ : _____   _____ : _____

_____ : _____   _____ : _____

_____ : _____   _____ : _____

P　Read the story about 林汉理, then answer the questions.

　　林汉理是十年级四班的学生。他是一个好
学生，上课不迟到(chídào)，不说话，很注意听(zhùyì tīng)，喜欢
问问题(wèntí)。他作业都做得很好，考试也考得很好，
尤其(yóuqí)是数学，常常考一百分。

　　林汉理最大的问题(wèntí)是很"健忘(jiànwàng)"。他常常买
东西忘了带(dài)钱，借(jiè)东西忘了还(huán)，去学校忘了带(dài)作业，上游泳课忘了带(dài)游泳
衣。他妈妈说："如果(rúguǒ)你写下来的话，你就会记得(jìde)。"林汉理说："我知道(zhīdao)，
可是我都忘了写下来。如果(rúguǒ)写下来的话，我也会忘了看。"

1. How does 林汉理 behave in the class and how is his schoolwork?

2. What does "健忘" mean?

3. What problems does 林汉理 often encounter?

4. What advice was given to him and by whom?

5. Would the advice work? Give reasons.

dì èr kè　　zěnme qù
第 二 课　怎 么 去 ……

A Early in the morning, every member of 小英 Xiǎoyīng's family is busy starting their day. Describe the mode of transport each person uses.

_____

_____

_____

_____

B Answer the following questions about 小英 Xiǎoyīng's family according to the information given on the previous page.

1. 小英坐公共汽车上学吗？

_____

2. 小英的弟弟坐游览车去动物园吗？
　　　　　 yóulǎnchē　　　 dòngwùyuán

_____

3. 小英的爸爸开车去科学馆上班吗？
　　　　　 kāi

_____

4. 小英的妹妹坐火车去学校吗？

_____

5. 从小英家到科学馆有多远？

_____

6. 小英家离医院有多远？
　　　　 yīyuàn

_____

7. 从小英家坐火车到美术馆要多长时间？

_____

8. 小英的哥哥骑摩托车到银行要多长时间？
　　　　　　 mótuōchē　　　 yínháng

_____

C Answer the following questions about yourself. Provide as much information as possible.

1. 你走路上学吗？

_____

2. 你爸爸<ruby>开车<rt>kāichē</rt></ruby>送你上学吗？

_____

3. 你家离学校有多远？

_____

4. 从你家走路到学校要多长时间？

_____

5. 从你家骑车到学校要多长时间？

_____

6. 他家离学校远吗？

7. 她坐公共汽车上学吗？

8. 他今天早上怎么了？

D Interview your friends to find out how they travel to school, including: 1. distance from home to school, 2. whether (they think) it is far, 3. mode of transport, 4. length of time required to get to school.

The four questions you need for your interview:

1. _____

2. _____

3. _____

4. _____

Fill in the information you obtain and report the results of your interview to your class.

Name				

Your findings: 1. Percentage of homes that are more than five kilometers away from school.

2. Percentage of people who think that the school is far from their home.

3. Most common mode of transport used.

4. Number of people whose travel time is more than 20 minutes.

二十

E Choose an appropriate word for each sentence, then use that word to write a sentence of your own.

左右	多远	几	多长	不到	只	jiāngjìn 将近

1. 你家离火车站有_____？

_____

2. 我家离火车站很远，_____十公里。

_____

3. 我家离学校很近，_____一公里。

_____

4. 我家离动物园四十公里 _____。
（dòngwùyuán）

_____

5. 从你家走路到美术馆要 _____时间？

_____

6. 从我家走路到美术馆要三十 _____分钟。

_____

7. 从我家骑车到学校 _____要五分钟。

_____

F Answer the following questions according to the information given on the map.

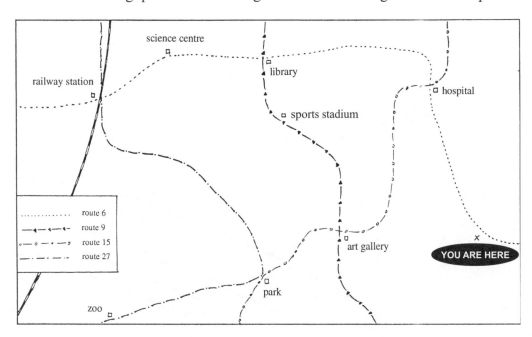

1. 请问到医院要坐几路车？
   _{yīyuàn}

   _____

2. 从医院到美术馆要坐几路车？
   _{yīyuàn}

   _____

3. 从美术馆到体育馆要不要换车？
   _{tǐyùguǎn}　_{huàn}

   _____

4. 从体育馆到科学馆要不要换车？怎么换车？
   _{tǐyùguǎn}　_{huàn}

   _____

5. 从科学馆到动物园要换几路车？
   _{dòngwùyuán}

   _____

G Answer the following questions according to the information given on the map.

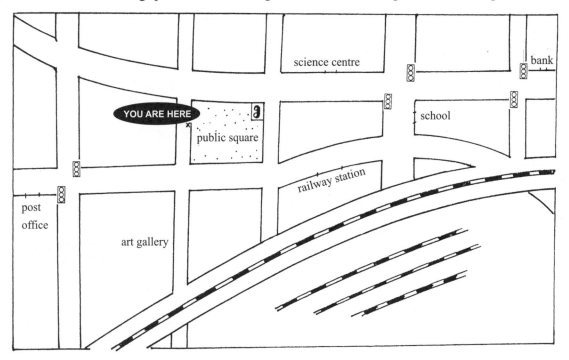

1. 请问到火车站怎么走？

_____

2. 请问到学校怎么走？

_____

3. 请问电话亭(tíng)在哪儿？怎么走？

_____

4. 到银行(yínháng)要过几个十字路口？

_____

5. 到邮局(yóujú)要不要过红绿灯路口？

_____

H Rearrange the characters in each question to make a sentence/conversation.

1. 走上你学吗路？不，我自学车上骑行。

_____

2. 我爸班公共坐车上汽爸。

_____

3. 小离英家校多有学远？很近，不一里公到。

_____

4. 你车在口坐校门七路，在科馆站学车下。

_____

5. 你从儿往这走前，过个红一绿口就灯路是。

_____

6. 从这坐火儿车到北多长时京要间？只几要十分。

_____

7. 北有多京儿离这远？两多公五千百里。

_____

8. 我想路去儿东买点西过马吃。

_____

I Rewrite the following in Chinese, using as many characters as possible.

1. Do you know which bus to take?

_____

2. Do I need to change buses?

_____

3. Which bus do I need to change to?

_____

4. Do you know which stop to get off at?

_____

5. (May I ask) how do I get to the railway station?

_____

6. Do I need to cross the traffic light intersection?

_____

7. Do you know how to get to the art gallery?

_____

8. Do you know where the telephone booth is?

_____

J Combine the characters in the box to make as many words or expressions as you can.

共 校 公 马 绿 口 门 东 西 火 面 站 不 过 汽 自 行
骑 坐 长 里 车 红 路 灯 色 多 时 间 少 学 久 小 远

words/expressions　　meaning　　　　words/expressions　　meaning

_____ : _____　　_____ : _____

_____ : _____　　_____ : _____

_____ : _____　　_____ : _____

_____ : _____　　_____ : _____

_____ : _____　　_____ : _____

_____ : _____　　_____ : _____

_____ : _____　　_____ : _____

_____ : _____　　_____ : _____

K Imagine you are 白大伟 Bái Dàwěi and write about your excursion in your diary. You may include the visit to the temple, your lunch and what happened after lunch.

L Listen to the conversation between 小兰 Xiǎolán and 小丽 Xiǎolì; then answer the following questions.

1. Where is 小兰 Xiǎolán going? Why is she in such a hurry?

2. What mode of transport is 小兰 Xiǎolán going to take? Why did she choose it?

3. What is the distance to 小兰 Xiǎolán's destination? How long will it take her to get there?

4. What advice did 小丽 Xiǎolì give 小兰 Xiǎolán?

In the box below, paste the copy of the conversation given to you by your teacher to further check your understanding. Use this copy to hold a conversation with your partner.

M Read the story about 林汉理, then answer the questions.

　　林汉理的学校离他家不远，差不多七公里。从他家到学校，坐火车只要五分钟，坐公共汽车要二十五分钟，骑车要三十几分。林汉理不坐火车上学，也不坐公共汽车上学，他骑车上学。

　　林汉理的学校在南边，可是林汉理每天早上不往南骑，他往东骑。他每天早上七点二十分往东骑三公里左右，到朋友陈英家，再和陈英一起骑

车到陈英的学校。陈英的学校在她家东南边，离她家有四公里。他们到了陈英的学校后，林汉理再往西南骑六公里到他自己的学校。他到学校的时间是八点三十五分。

1. To go to school, what choices of transport does 林汉理 have and which one does he choose?

2. Draw a diagram of the route 林汉理 takes to school every day, including the direction and the distance.

3. How long should it take 林汉理 to ride to school and how long does it actually take him? Explain the reason.

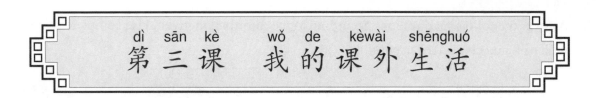

A Based on the TV guide on page 45 in the Textbook, answer the following questions.

1. 今天有没有动画片^{dònghuàpiān}？是第几频道^{píndào}的？

_____

2. 今天有没有体育^{tǐyù}节目？是哪几个频道^{píndào}的？

_____

3. 今天哪几个频道^{píndào}有连续剧^{liánxùjù}？

_____

4. 今天哪几个频道^{píndào}有电影？

_____

5. 第八频道^{píndào}有没有儿童^{értóng}节目？从几点到几点？

_____

6. 第六频道^{píndào}有没有教育^{jiàoyù}节目？从几点到几点？

_____

7. 今天下午七点半有没有新闻^{xīnwén}？在第几频道^{píndào}？

_____

8. 今天的电视，你最喜欢哪个节目？

_____

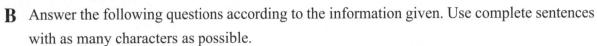

B Answer the following questions according to the information given. Use complete sentences with as many characters as possible.

1. 你这个周末怎么过？^{zhōumò}

_____

2. 你今天晚上想不想去看电影？

_____

3. 这部电影是武侠片吗？^{bù　　　wǔxiá}

_____

4. 这是一部历史片还是恐怖片？^{bù　　　kǒngbù}

_____

5. 你喜欢爱情片还是科幻片？^{àiqíng　　　kēhuàn}

_____

6. 你喜欢恐怖片吗？为什么？^{kǒngbù}

_____

7. 你喜欢侦探片吗？为什么？^{zhēntàn}

_____

8. 你明天自己一个人去看电影吗？

me　younger brother

_____

C Listen to the conversation and draw lines connecting the person to the type of entertainment he/she enjoys.

Chris　　Jenny　　　Thomas　　Lily　　　Charles　　Karen　　　Jim　　　Clair

Describe the type of entertainment the above people enjoy, using complete sentences with as many characters as possible.

_____

_____

_____

_____

_____

D Choose an appropriate word for each sentence, then use that word to write a sentence of your own.

| 每　　就　　不是　　就是　　又 |

1. 她今天一整天_____吃东西，就是睡觉。
（yìzhěngtiān）（shuìjiào）

_____

2. 他 _____ 个周末都去看电影。
（zhōumò）

_____

3. 我 _____ 知道你喜欢我妹妹。

_____

4. 他今天什么事都没做，_____看电视。

_____

E Rewrite the following sentences in Chinese using 又……又…….

1. These grapes are big and sweet.

_____

2. Those dresses are expensive and not good-looking.

_____

3. That movie is tense and exciting.

_____

F　Answer the following questions about yourself. Use complete sentences with as many characters as possible.

1. 你对<ruby>摇滚乐<rt>yáogǔnyuè</rt></ruby>有没有<ruby>兴趣<rt>xìngqù</rt></ruby>？为什么？

_____

2. 你对京剧有没有<ruby>兴趣<rt>xìngqù</rt></ruby>？为什么？

_____

3. 你对什么音乐有<ruby>兴趣<rt>xìngqù</rt></ruby>？

_____

4. 你听<ruby>交响乐<rt>jiāoxiǎngyuè</rt></ruby>吗？为什么？

_____

5. 你常打球吗？打什么球？

_____

6. 你喜欢打篮球还是打网球？

_____

7. 你喜欢看球赛吗？你是不是个球迷？

_____

8. 你常看电视吗？你是不是个电视迷？

_____

G Compare the following, using 比较 bǐjiào (no. 1-5) and 更 gèng (no. 6-8). Write in complete sentences with as many characters as possible.

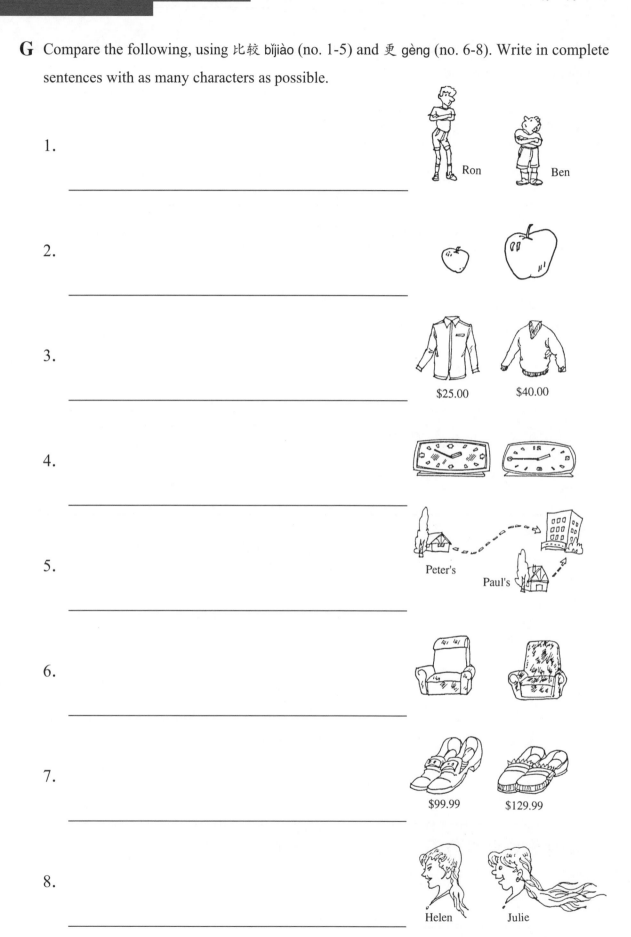

1. _____

2. _____

3. _____

4. _____

5. _____

6. _____

7. _____

8. _____

H Interview nine friends about their leisure time. Find out about: 1. what TV programs they like, 2. what type of movies they like, 3. what sort of music they enjoy, 4. what sports they enjoy playing.

The four questions you need for the interview:

1. _____

2. _____

3. _____

4. _____

Fill in the information you obtain and report the results of your interview to your class.

Name				
Your conclusion				

I Write the following performances in Chinese.

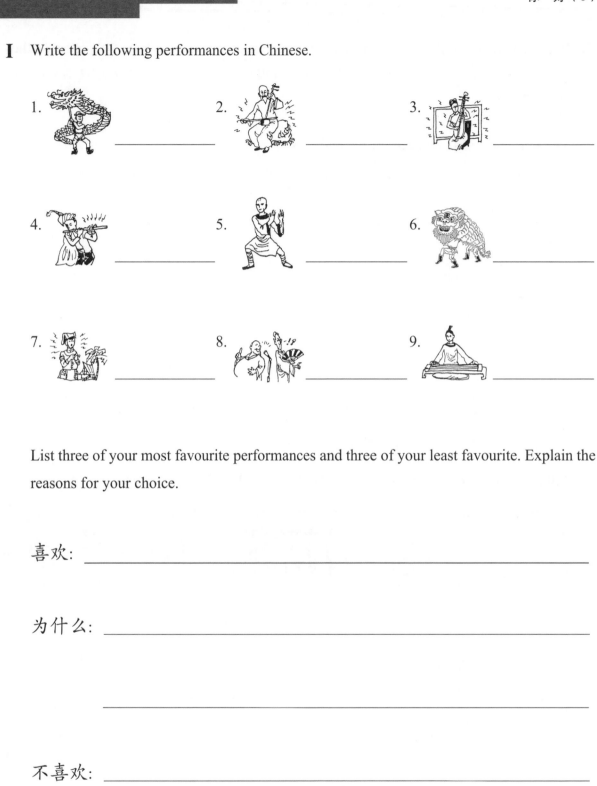

1. ＿＿＿＿＿＿＿

2. ＿＿＿＿＿＿＿

3. ＿＿＿＿＿＿＿

4. ＿＿＿＿＿＿＿

5. ＿＿＿＿＿＿＿

6. ＿＿＿＿＿＿＿

7. ＿＿＿＿＿＿＿

8. ＿＿＿＿＿＿＿

9. ＿＿＿＿＿＿＿

List three of your most favourite performances and three of your least favourite. Explain the reasons for your choice.

喜欢: ＿＿＿＿＿＿＿＿＿＿＿＿＿＿＿＿＿＿＿＿＿＿＿＿＿＿＿＿＿＿

为什么: ＿＿＿＿＿＿＿＿＿＿＿＿＿＿＿＿＿＿＿＿＿＿＿＿＿＿＿＿

＿＿＿＿＿＿＿＿＿＿＿＿＿＿＿＿＿＿＿＿＿＿＿＿＿＿＿＿

不喜欢: ＿＿＿＿＿＿＿＿＿＿＿＿＿＿＿＿＿＿＿＿＿＿＿＿＿＿＿＿

为什么: ＿＿＿＿＿＿＿＿＿＿＿＿＿＿＿＿＿＿＿＿＿＿＿＿＿＿＿＿

＿＿＿＿＿＿＿＿＿＿＿＿＿＿＿＿＿＿＿＿＿＿＿＿＿＿＿＿

J Combine the characters in the box to make as many words or expressions as you can.

电 节 篮 视 迷 路 票 车 球 足 赛 宜 小 歌 便 京 北
唱 姐 走 大 很 影 天 气 生 网 剧 音 排 话 乐 每 目

words/expressions	meaning	words/expressions	meaning
_____ : _____		_____ : _____	
_____ : _____		_____ : _____	
_____ : _____		_____ : _____	
_____ : _____		_____ : _____	
_____ : _____		_____ : _____	
_____ : _____		_____ : _____	
_____ : _____		_____ : _____	
_____ : _____		_____ : _____	
_____ : _____		_____ : _____	

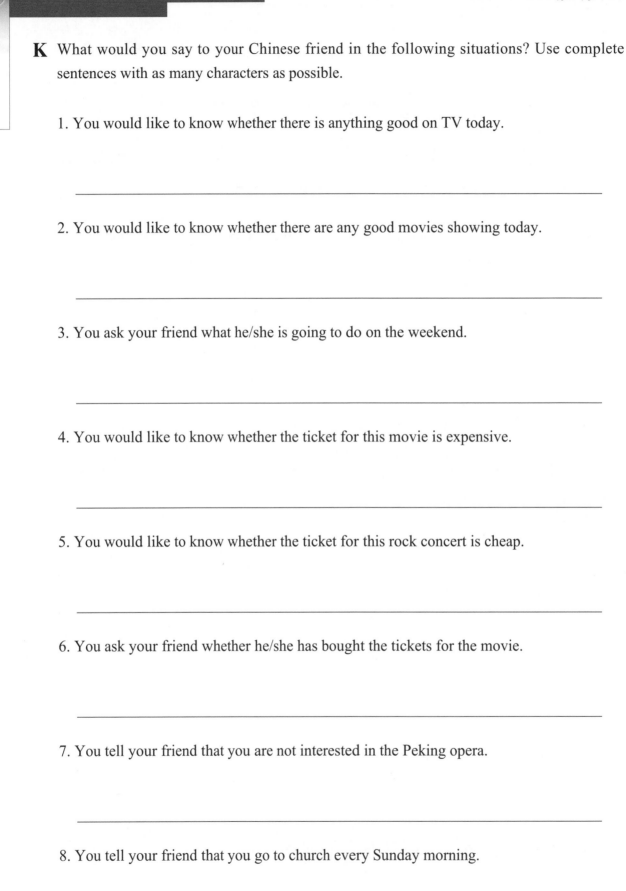

K What would you say to your Chinese friend in the following situations? Use complete sentences with as many characters as possible.

1. You would like to know whether there is anything good on TV today.

_____

2. You would like to know whether there are any good movies showing today.

_____

3. You ask your friend what he/she is going to do on the weekend.

_____

4. You would like to know whether the ticket for this movie is expensive.

_____

5. You would like to know whether the ticket for this rock concert is cheap.

_____

6. You ask your friend whether he/she has bought the tickets for the movie.

_____

7. You tell your friend that you are not interested in the Peking opera.

_____

8. You tell your friend that you go to church every Sunday morning.

_____

L　Rearrange the characters in each question to make a sentence.

1. 今视节天有什看的么好电目？

_____

2. 我哥个日都星期去打球篮哥每。

_____

3. 明不是天我去游去打泳就是网球。

_____

4. 他是迷足球弟弟，每期六去看都球个星赛。

_____

5. 那影电场很宜便，我票三张买了。
chǎng

_____

6. 他欢喜听京爸爸剧，不喜影欢看电。

_____

7. 那件服衣又又贵不看好。

_____

8. 昨上的音天晚乐会，我姐了两姐唱歌首。
shǒu

_____

M Listen to the conversation between 小兰 Xiǎolán and 小丽 Xiǎolì; then answer the following questions.

1. Where do you think this conversation took place?

2. What was the purpose of this conversation?

3. What activities did every member of 小丽 Xiǎolì's family do?

4. What activity did 小丽 Xiǎolì suggest and what was 小兰 Xiǎolán's decision?

In the box below, paste the copy of the conversation given to you by your teacher to further check your understanding. Use this copy to hold a conversation with your partner.

N Read the story about 林汉理 and 陈英, then answer the questions.

今天，林汉理请陈英去看电影。林汉理喜欢

看侦探片和恐怖片，可是陈英不喜欢，所以他们去

看了一部爱情片。林汉理觉得这部电影没什么

意思，可是陈英感动得哭了。

　　看过电影，陈英说她想买一本汉英字典，所以他们坐火车去了中国

城。中国城离电影院不近，大约二十公里左右，可是坐火车只要十几分钟。

今天中国城的书店外面有人在唱京剧，陈英说他们唱得不错，只是林汉理

一点都听不懂。买了字典，陈英说："你看，对面有人在拉二胡，我们过

去听吧！"林汉理对二胡没兴趣，他说："时间不早了，我看，我们该回

去了。"

1. What type of movie did they see and how did each of them enjoy it?

2. Where did they go after the movie and why did they go there?

3. How far away was that place and how did they get there?

4. Do you think both of them enjoyed their day? Justify your answer.

dì　sì　kè　　fùxí
第 四 课　复 习 （ 一 ）

A What would you say in the following situations? Use complete sentences with as many characters as possible.

1. You explain to your friend that you are late because of the heavy rain.

_____

2. You explain to your teacher that you are late because you missed the train.

_____

3. You tell your friend that you like science, and you did very well in the last test.

_____

4. You tell your friend that you like history, but you did badly in last week's test.

_____

5. You tell a visitor that the zoo is very far from here and he needs to change buses.

_____

6. You would like to know which bus goes to the museum and where to catch it.

_____

7. You ask your friend whether he/she is going to see tonight's football match.

_____

8. You would like to know the admission fee for next Sunday's concert.

_____

B Combine the characters in the box to make as many words or expressions as you can.

雨 课 班 车 科 因 学 同 生 喜 日 票 买 路 门 走 马
上 数 来 口 起 考 下 试 坐 为 校 以 早 本 欢 骑 一

words/expressions　　meaning　　　　words/expressions　　meaning

_____ : _____　　_____ : _____

_____ : _____　　_____ : _____

_____ : _____　　_____ : _____

_____ : _____　　_____ : _____

_____ : _____　　_____ : _____

_____ : _____　　_____ : _____

_____ : _____　　_____ : _____

_____ : _____　　_____ : _____

C This is an email 林汉理 received from a friend in Beijing. Read the mail and answer the questions.

汉理: 你好！

　　今天我们全家人去看了一部武侠电影，是李小龙演的。我妈妈觉得不怎么样，我爸爸说还不错，我觉得真是太棒了。这部电影很有意思，李小龙的功夫又好，我看得真过瘾。你现在常看电影吗？都看什么电影？和谁一起去看？

　　我的新学校离我们家很近，不到两公里，走路只要十四分钟左右。我每天走路上学。现在学校的功课很忙，每天作业都很多，尤其是数学和英语。我数学还好，最讨厌的是我们英语老师了，她还一天到晚考试，我考试都考得很糟。你的功课忙不忙？学校离你家远吗？你走路上学还是你爸爸开车送你上学？

业新

1. What recreation did the writer have today?

2. Who did he go with and how did everyone enjoy it?

3. How is his new school and how does he cope with his study?

4. What did he want to know about 林汉理?

D Imagine you are 林汉理, write a reply email to your friend in Beijing. Provide as much information about 林汉理 as you can, including your own additions.

E Rearrange the characters in each question to make a sentence/conversation.

1. 你昨地天的理考么样得怎？我得还考错不。

_____

2. 你学作数业做吗了？有没，我做了忘。

_____

3. 从校走学路半到美时左术馆要个小右。

_____

4. 从这长时儿骑到自馆要行车科学多间？

_____

5. 我学家离远的校挺，我车共汽上坐公学。

_____

6. 北京站火车前面个绿红灯有三路口。

_____

7. 他欢看目最喜的电是足视节球赛。

_____

8. 这便个球又篮好又宜。

_____

F Listen to the conversation between 小兰 Xiǎolán and her mother; then answer the following questions.

1. What time did 小兰 Xiǎolán's mother wake her up?

2. What's the weather like?

3. Where is 小兰 Xiǎolán's mother going?

4. What mode of transport are they going to take today?

In the box below, paste the copy of the conversation given to you by your teacher to further check your understanding. Use this copy to hold a conversation with your partner.

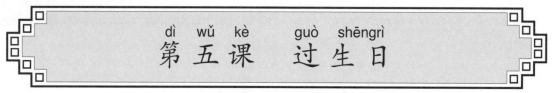

dì   wǔ   kè   guò   shēngrì
第 五 课　过 生 日

A Your birthday is coming up soon. Write an invitation to your Chinese friends. Use as many characters as possible.

Your school is having a fete (游园会 *yóuyuánhuì*). Write an invitation to students in a nearby school, inviting them to join in the fun.

B You are invited by your Chinese friend to join his/her birthday celebration, but you are unable to go. Write a thank-you note and explain the reason why you cannot go.

Your class is invited to attend a Chinese community's New Year celebration. Write a thank-you note and say that you will all be delighted to go.

五十

C Answer the following questions in complete sentences, with as many characters as possible.

1.这礼物是谁送的？

_____

2.他送她什么礼物？

_____

3.他爸爸送他什么生日礼物？

_____

4.你妈妈要在这儿住多久？

March 15 ➡ May 31

_____

5.你哥哥要在北京住多久？

S	M	T	W	T	F	S
					1	2
3	4	5	6	7	8	9
10	11	12	13	14	15	16
17	18	19	20	21	22	23
24	25	26	27	28	29	30

_____

6.你爸爸的生日，你要送他什么礼物？

_____

7.在你家，谁陪妈妈去买东西？

_____

8.你买东西时，找谁一块儿去？

_____

D Use 比 bǐ to compare the two in each question. The comparison should be a complete sentence with as many characters as possible.

1. _____

Lanlan　　Meiyi

2. _____

Vicky　　Karen

3. _____

April's　　Mary's

4. _____

Robert　　Richard

5. _____

¥199.00　　¥200.00

6. _____

Tony's　　Tom's

7. _____

Kay's　　Lynn's

8. _____

Nick　Scott

E Use 长得 zhǎng de to describe/compare the following in each question. The description should be a complete sentence with as many characters as possible.

1.

_____

Andy　　Alan

2.

_____

3.

_____

father　　Dennis

4.

_____

Emma　(twins)　Dianna

5.

_____

Carol

6.

_____

Agnes　younger sister

7.

_____

Mother　　Ann

8.

_____

Lily　　Lanlan

F Interview your friends to find out whether they have 1. eaten 粽子 zòngzi, 2. eaten 月饼 yuèbǐng, 3. been to China, 4. been to the United States.

The four questions you need for the interview:

1. _____

2. _____

3. _____

4. _____

Fill in the information you obtain and report the results of your interview to your class.

Name				

G Answer the following questions about yourself. Use complete sentences with as many characters as possible.

1. 你吃过粽子吗？在哪儿吃的？

_____

2. 你吃过月饼吗？谁请你吃的？

_____

3. 你去过动物园吗？去过哪个动物园？
   dòngwùyuán

_____

4. 你去过中国馆子吗？

_____

5. 你会自己做饭吗？会做什么菜？

_____

6. 你请同学吃饭吗？请过谁？

_____

7. 在你们家，谁做菜最拿手？

_____

8. 你喜欢喝什么饮料？
   yǐnliào

_____

H Imagine you are 王小明 Wáng Xiǎomíng and you just had your birthday party today. Write about your day in your diary.

I Combine the characters in the box to make as many words or expressions as you can.

| 拿 | 址 | 理 | 台 | 地 | 北 | 快 | 音 | 节 | 一 | 儿 | 会 | 子 | 包 | 后 | 粽 | 秋 |
| 乐 | 目 | 天 | 来 | 手 | 可 | 中 | 是 | 以 | 已 | 饺 | 面 | 春 | 每 | 能 | 经 | 住 |

words/expressions　　meaning　　　　　　words/expressions　　meaning

_____ : _____　　　　_____ : _____

_____ : _____　　　　_____ : _____

_____ : _____　　　　_____ : _____

_____ : _____　　　　_____ : _____

_____ : _____　　　　_____ : _____

_____ : _____　　　　_____ : _____

_____ : _____　　　　_____ : _____

_____ : _____　　　　_____ : _____

_____ : _____　　　　_____ : _____

J   What would you say to your Chinese friend in the following situations? Use complete sentences with as many characters as possible.

1. Ask your friend who gave him/her the computer.

_____

2. Ask your friend what his/her father is going to give him/her for his/her birthday.

_____

3. Say that your younger sister is taller than your mother.

_____

4. Tell your friend that you are much taller than him/her.

_____

5. Tell your friend that your father has been to the U.S.A. and Canada.

_____

6. Ask your friend whether he/she has been to Taiwan.

_____

7. Tell your friend that you have never eaten Chinese moon cakes.

_____

8. Say that you have not seen someone for a long time.

_____

K Rearrange the characters in each question to make a sentence/conversation.

1. 明的天我生是日，我请你我起家和想我一过到生日。

_____

2. 她请友了几个朋星饺期六她到家包子。

_____

3. 你礼要她什送么生日物？我送本她一小想说。

_____

4. 我我弟弟和长一点不得儿都像。

_____

5. 这比件服那件便衣多了宜。

_____

6. 你北去台吗过？没我过去。

_____

7. 你去哪些过中方国地？我过北只去京。

_____

8. 我看去电们先影，看了影再电去泳游。

_____

L Listen to the conversation between 李秋 Lǐ Qiū and the person she came across; then answer the following questions.

1. Who was the person 李秋 Lǐ Qiū mistook for 大伟 Dàwěi? Why did she make this mistake?

2. Compare the appearance of this person with 大伟 Dàwěi's.

3. What is 李秋 Lǐ Qiū's destination?

4. What transport is 李秋 Lǐ Qiū taking?

In the box below, paste the copy of the conversation given to you by your teacher to further check your understanding. Use this copy to hold a conversation with your partner.

M Read the story about 林汉理 and 陈英, then answer the questions.

今年中秋节，林汉理的爸爸和妈妈去北京看朋友，家里只有他一个

人，^{Chén}陈英就请他到她们家一起过节。

陈英的妈妈很会做菜，她做了古老肉^{gǔlǎoròu}、狮子头^{shīzitóu}和豆腐汤^{dòufu tāng}，都是林汉理

喜欢的，他吃得很过瘾^{guòyǐn}。吃过饭后，他们在院子^{yuànzi}

里喝茶，吃月饼。吃过月饼，陈英带林汉理到对

面的公园散步^{sànbù}。林汉理说："你和你妈妈长得真

像，鼻子^{bízi}挺挺^{tǐng}的，嘴巴^{zuǐba}小小的，眼睛^{yǎnjing}大大的。你

妈妈真年轻^{niánqīng}，看起来就像是你姐姐。"陈英说：

"怎么会呢？我妈妈比我矮多了，又有白头发。

我觉得她看起来比我老多了。"

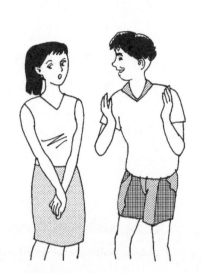

1. Why was 林汉理 invited and how was he received?

2. What comment did he make on 陈英 's appearance?

3. What does " 年轻 " mean?

4. What was 陈英 's reaction to his comment?

dì liù kè   wǒ bìng le
第 六 课　我 病 了

A Describe what symptoms these people have. Use complete sentences with as many characters as possible.

1. _____

2. _____

_____

3. _____

_____

4. _____

_____

B Rewrite the following in Chinese, using as many characters as possible.

1. How did this happen? My money is gone.

_____

2. What happened to you? Where do you feel sick?

_____

3. Are you alright?

_____

4. I have to go to the toilet.

_____

C Answer the following questions according to the information given.

1. 他怎么了？

_____

2. 他哪里不舒服？

_____

3. 他的<ruby>体温<rt>tǐwēn</rt></ruby>现在多少度？他发烧吗？

39°6

_____

4. 他<ruby>咳嗽<rt>késòu</rt></ruby>吗？

_____

5. 他要去哪里？

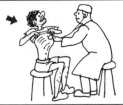

_____

6. 你看他是不是感冒了？

_____

7. 你看他是不是吃坏了肚子？

_____

8. 他今天在哪儿吃了<ruby>刨冰<rt>bàobīng</rt></ruby>？

_____

D Listen to the conversation and choose the illness/symptom that is mentioned.

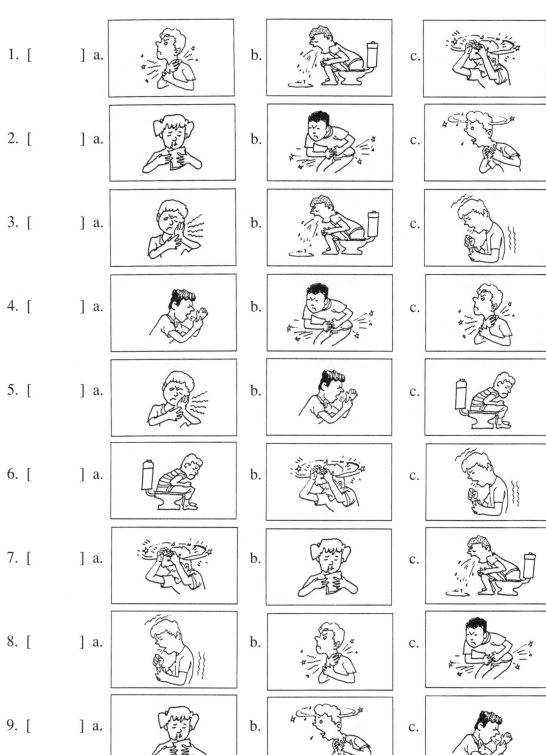

1. [　　] a.　　　b.　　　c.

2. [　　] a.　　　b.　　　c.

3. [　　] a.　　　b.　　　c.

4. [　　] a.　　　b.　　　c.

5. [　　] a.　　　b.　　　c.

6. [　　] a.　　　b.　　　c.

7. [　　] a.　　　b.　　　c.

8. [　　] a.　　　b.　　　c.

9. [　　] a.　　　b.　　　c.

10. [　　] a.　　　b.　　　c.

E Your Chinese friend did not feel well. He went to the doctor and bought some medicine. Write a note to explain to him how he should take it. Use complete sentences with as many characters as possible.

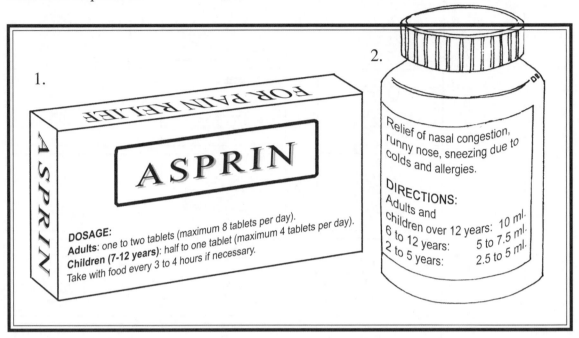

1.
_____

_____

_____

2.
_____

_____

_____

F Your friend went to a Chinese doctor and was given the following medicine. Explain in English how he is to take it.

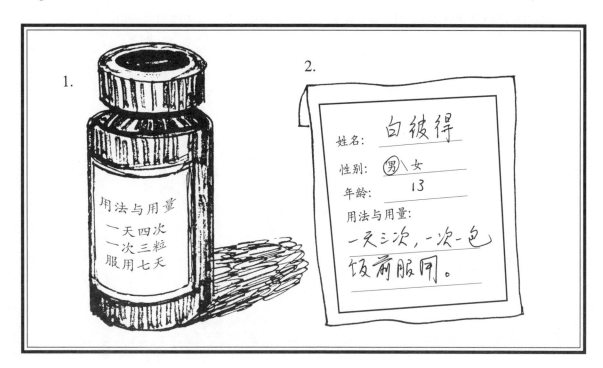

1. _____

_____

_____

2. _____

_____

_____

G Work in pairs with your partner to create a conversation. One of you has the flu and the other is a doctor. Your conversation should include a discussion about symptoms and instructions on taking the medication. Use as many characters as possible.

D: _____

P: _____

D: _____

P: _____

D: _____

P: _____

D: _____

P: _____

D: _____

第六课　我病了

P: _____

H You do not feel well this morning. Your mother suggests that you should take the day off from school and she will take you to the doctor later. Draft a note to your teacher for your mother to sign and ask your Chinese classmate next door to take the note to school for you.

Note to your teacher:

_____

_____

_____

_____

_____

Write here what you are going to tell your Chinese classmate next door:

_____

_____

_____

_____

I Influenza is going around and many people caught it before the end of the previous week. Back at school on Monday, there is a conversation about the subject. Listen to the conversation and draw lines joining each person with the proper description.

Peter	has had it for three days	not better at all.
Margaret	has had it for nearly a week	a little better
John	has had it for one day	much better
Clare	does not remember how many days	still coughs
Alan	did not catch the flu	had to visit the doctor
Helen	has had it for more than a week	feels tired

Check your answer and describe each person's situation in your own words. Write in complete sentences with as many characters as possible.

Peter:

_____

Margaret:

_____

John:

_____

Clare:

_____

Alan:

_____

Helen:

_____

J Combine the characters in the box to make as many words or expressions as you can.

生 衣 假 医 疼 厕 面 以 喝 张 水 茶 汽 所 票 舒 子
服 拉 牙 肚 冒 气 病 天 后 头 包 休 车 息 感 开 条

words/expressions　　meaning　　　　words/expressions　　meaning

_____ : _____　　_____ : _____

_____ : _____　　_____ : _____

_____ : _____　　_____ : _____

_____ : _____　　_____ : _____

_____ : _____　　_____ : _____

_____ : _____　　_____ : _____

_____ : _____　　_____ : _____

_____ : _____　　_____ : _____

K What would you say in Chinese in the following situations? Use complete sentences with as many characters as possible.

1. Tell your teacher that you do not feel well and you probably have a temperature.

_____

2. Tell your friend that you vomitted and had diarrhoea last night.

_____

3. Say that you have a cold and a sore throat.

_____

4. Tell your friend the reason he has a toothache is because he eats too much chocolate (巧克力 qiǎokèlì).

_____

5. Your friend was sick yesterday. Ask him/her whether he/she is feeling better today.

_____

6. Tell your teacher that you have a stomach-ache and ask for the afternoon off.

_____

7. Your friend does not look well. Ask him/her whether he/she is alright.

_____

8. Tell your class that your English teacher cannot come to class because he was injured in a car accident.

_____

L Rearrange the characters in each question to make a sentence/conversation.

1. 我服舒天今不，想里休在家息。

---

2. 我怎么们的美师术老了？他了病，今不天课来上。

---

3. 病了我，妈妈写了假条一张给帮我老师。

---

4. 你没上怎么学弟弟？牙疼他，我去看妈他妈带牙医。

---

5. 这是药感冒，你一三天吃次，一两片次。

---

6. 他吃坏昨天了子肚，天今上泻下吐。

---

7. 你的病爸爸儿了好点吗？些好了。

---

8. 她喝水只，不都吃东西什么。

M Listen to the conversation; then answer the following questions.

1. Where did the conversation take place?

2. What happened to 小丽 Xiǎolì?

3. What did 小丽 Xiǎolì feel like doing?

4. What was the teacher's response to 小丽 Xiǎolì's request?

In the box below, paste the copy of conversation given to you by your teacher to further check your understanding. Use this copy to hold a conversation with your partner.

N Read the story about 陈英, then answer the questions.

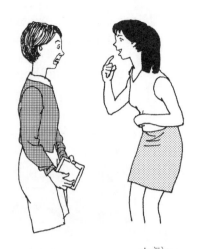

陈英感冒了，三天没去上课。她前天发高烧，一整天都在睡觉；昨天还有点发烧，一整天都在咳嗽；今天好多了，已经不发烧了，只是还有点儿咳嗽。

今天下课后，林汉理骑车来看她，还买了一包巧克力送给她。这包巧克力一共有十二块，陈英晚饭前吃了四块，吃饭时吃了两块，饭后又吃了三块。睡觉前，陈英肚子不舒服。她妈妈说："因为你吃了太多巧克力，所以肚子不舒服。"

陈英说："不！你看，我的感冒已经好了。就是因为我吃了巧克力，所以现在不咳嗽了。"

1. What illness did 陈英 have and how did the symptoms progress?

2. What present did she receive and what did she do to it?

3. What consequence did she have and how did she justify it?

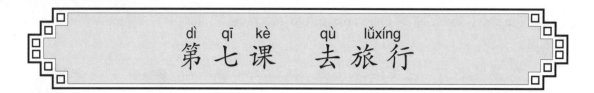

dì qī kè   qù lǚxíng
第 七 课　去 旅 行

A These people are talking about plans for their next trip. Draw a line joining each person to his/her destination.

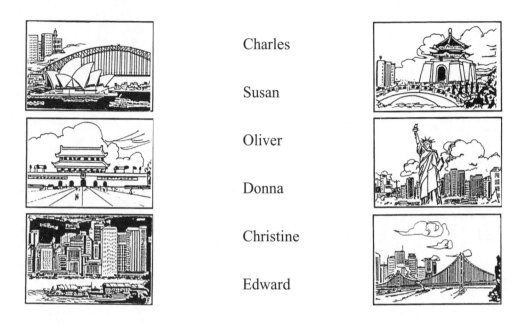

Charles

Susan

Oliver

Donna

Christine

Edward

Write the plans of the people above. Use complete sentences.

1. _____

2. _____

3. _____

4. _____

5. _____

6. _____

B Answer the following questions about yourself. Use complete sentences with as many characters as possible.

1. 你暑假^{shǔjià}打算做什么？

_____

2. 你寒假^{hánjià}打算去哪儿玩？

_____

3. 你这个周末^{zhōumò}打算做什么？

_____

4. 你打算送你朋友什么生日礼物^{lǐwù}？

_____

5. 我打算明年去中国旅行，你呢？

_____

6. 明年你有什么新计划^{jìhuà}？

_____

7. 下午如果^{rúguǒ}不下雨的话，我打算去游泳。你去不去？

_____

8. 考试快到了，你有什么计划^{jìhuà}？

_____

C Choose an appropriate word for each sentence, then use that word to write a sentence of your own.

哪些	可能	打算	哪儿	旅行

1. 这次旅行，你打算去 ＿＿＿＿＿ 地方？

＿＿＿＿＿＿＿＿＿＿＿＿＿＿＿＿＿＿＿＿＿＿＿＿＿

2. 我看，明天 ＿＿＿＿＿ 会下雨。

＿＿＿＿＿＿＿＿＿＿＿＿＿＿＿＿＿＿＿＿＿＿＿＿＿

3. 他们 ＿＿＿＿＿ 暑假干什么？
<small>gàn</small>

＿＿＿＿＿＿＿＿＿＿＿＿＿＿＿＿＿＿＿＿＿＿＿＿＿

4. 我 ＿＿＿＿＿ 都不去。

＿＿＿＿＿＿＿＿＿＿＿＿＿＿＿＿＿＿＿＿＿＿＿＿＿

D Rewrite the following sentences in Chinese using 都不.

1. I am not going anywhere today.

＿＿＿＿＿＿＿＿＿＿＿＿＿＿＿＿＿＿＿＿＿＿＿＿＿

2. I am not doing anything tomorrow.

＿＿＿＿＿＿＿＿＿＿＿＿＿＿＿＿＿＿＿＿＿＿＿＿＿

3. She doesn't want to eat anything.

＿＿＿＿＿＿＿＿＿＿＿＿＿＿＿＿＿＿＿＿＿＿＿＿＿

E Your Chinese friend is visiting you, and you are to arrange a sightseeing trip. Find a suitable trip in a newspaper or a tourist brochure and write down the information for him/her. Use as many characters as possible.

地点：

_____

时间：

_____

^{fèiyòng}
费用：

_____

^{xíngchéng}
行程：

_____

_____

_____

_____

_____

_____

F　Compare the photograph with the person him/herself. Use complete sentences with as many characters as possible.

1.

_____

Irene

2.

_____

Bob

3.

_____

Jack

4.

_____

Xiaoming

5.

_____

Cathy

6.

_____

Jim

7.

_____

Linda

8.

_____

Tracy

G Sharon is asking Peter about the trip he is taking. Answer Sharon's questions for Peter. Use complete sentences with as many characters as possible.

1. 这次旅行你打算去哪些地方？

_____

2. 你打算和谁一块儿去？

Shelly
a friend

_____

3. 你计划去多久？
   jìhuà

_____

4. 你机票买了吗？

AIRPLANE

yes

_____

5. 你签证办好了没有？
   qiānzhèng

PASSPORT

no

_____

6. 你带照相机去吗？

I (✘)　　Shelly (√)

_____

7. 你的行李多不多？有几件？

_____

8. 你要我帮你收拾行李吗？
   shōushi

no need
packed

_____

H Rewrite the following in Chinese, using as many characters as possible.

1. I am going to the airport to see Mary off.

_____

2. Aren't you going to the airport to see her off too?

_____

3. Why didn't I see your little sister? Isn't she coming too?

_____

4. The flight departs at 11:25 a.m..

_____

5. I am sorry that I am late.

_____

6. There was a traffic jam on the way home this afternoon.

_____

7. Speak of the devil.

_____

8. Wish you a happy journey.

_____

I Combine the characters in the box to make as many words or expressions as you can.

旅	李	不	打	机	黄	飞	算	票	起	差	只	好	多	片	相	香
海	行	本	照	金	来	假	人	暑	度	少	色	病	条	港	岸	是

words/expressions　　　meaning　　　　　　words/expressions　　　meaning

_____ : _____　　_____ : _____

_____ : _____　　_____ : _____

_____ : _____　　_____ : _____

_____ : _____　　_____ : _____

_____ : _____　　_____ : _____

_____ : _____　　_____ : _____

_____ : _____　　_____ : _____

_____ : _____　　_____ : _____

J What would you say in Chinese in the following situations? Use complete sentences with as many characters as possible.

1. Ask your friend what he/she plans to do on the weekend.

_____

2. Tell your friend you will probably go to the movies on Sunday afternoon.

_____

3. Your teacher is carrying your class's notebooks. Ask her whether she needs a hand.

_____

4. Your friend is going to the tuck shop. Ask him/her to buy a sandwich for you.

_____

5. Tell your friend you went to the studio yesterday to be photographed with your father.

_____

6. Tell your Chinese pen friend that you are much better looking than in the photograph.

_____

7. Your class is going for an excursion tomorrow. Remind your friend to bring a camera.

_____

8. Tell your friend that you are going to the airport on Saturday to see your uncle off.

_____

K Rearrange the characters in each question to make a sentence/conversation.

1. 你去哪儿打算玩暑假？我都不哪儿去。

_____

2. 要我帮不要你买东点儿西？好，你帮一个我买照机相。

_____

3. 我打算爸爸下个带我们星期去黄金玩儿海岸。

_____

4. 你的飞飞机起时候什么？差五点分三。

_____

5. 你看个那人是男女的的还是？

_____

6. 她瘦很，可是得她她觉自己太了胖。

_____

7. 这旅行次我不算打带太西多东。

_____

8. 你不泳吗去游？不去，我看要去影电。

_____

八
十
四

L Listen to the conversation between 李秋 Lǐ Qiū and 兰兰 Lánlan; then answer the following questions.

1. Where is 兰兰 Lánlan's family going for a holiday and for how long?

2. What does 兰兰 Lánlan plan to do there?

3. What was the aim of 兰兰 Lánlan's conversation with 李秋 Lǐ Qiū?

4. What was the conclusion of their conversation?

In the box below, paste the copy of the conversation given to you by your teacher to further check your understanding. Use this copy to hold a conversation with your partner.

M Read the story about 陈英 's family, then answer the questions.

陈英的爸爸很喜欢旅行。他每次出去旅行都拍很多照片。这个周末，他爸爸开车带全家人去悉尼玩儿。

悉尼离他们家有三百二十五公里，开车要四个半小时。他们星期六上午九点从家里出发。到了悉尼，他们先吃午饭，吃过午饭，再去动物园。到了动物园，他爸爸说："我们等一会儿还要去歌剧院，在这儿只停留十五分钟，大家快下车拍照。"他们下了车，爸爸要大家站这边拍照，站那边拍照。拍了照，他说："好了，大家都上车，我们该走了。"陈英说："爸爸，我想多看看动物呢！"他爸爸说："不用看，回家看照片就行了。"

1. Where did they go and how long was the trip?

2. Describe their itinerary for the first day.

3. What do you think 陈英 's father enjoyed the most during the trip?

4. Do you think 陈英 likes her father's arrangement for the trip? Give reasons for your answer.

dì   bā   kè   fùxí
第 八 课　复 习 （ 二 ）

A What would you say in Chinese in the following situations? Use complete sentences with as many characters as possible.

1. Tell your friend that tomorrow is your mother's birthday and you don't know what to buy for her.

_____

2. Next Saturday is your birthday. Invite your friend over to celebrate with you.

_____

3. Say that your brother/sister is a little skinnier than you.

_____

4. Say that your father/mother is much fatter than you.

_____

5. Tell your teacher that you would like to go to Hong Kong when there is an opportunity.

_____

6. Say that you have been to Beijing and you have a good impression of the city.

_____

7. Tell your teacher that you have a headache and you need to go to the sick room.

_____

8. Say that your aunt is going to England and you are going to the airport to see her off.

_____

B Combine the characters in the box to make as many words or expressions as you can.

> 间 差 能 点 少 小 回 校 人 长 最 过 因 为 有 以 得
> 所 学 用 多 法 可 不 时 来 家 近 儿 子 地 理 觉 年

words/expressions	meaning	words/expressions	meaning
_____ : _____		_____ : _____	
_____ : _____		_____ : _____	
_____ : _____		_____ : _____	
_____ : _____		_____ : _____	
_____ : _____		_____ : _____	
_____ : _____		_____ : _____	
_____ : _____		_____ : _____	
_____ : _____		_____ : _____	
_____ : _____		_____ : _____	

C Rearrange the characters in each question to make a sentence/conversation.

1. 明他的天是生日，他我请到一他家起生日过。

_____

2. 小英天个请了朋友六星期到她包饺子家。

_____

3. 你你爸爸送礼物生日什么？他我送票电影一张。

_____

4. 他篮球弟弟是迷，星期六每个上午都篮球去看赛。

_____

5. 那很便场宜会音乐，我买一共张票了五。

_____

6. 中国年糕人吃过年，端午粽节吃子，中秋月饼节吃。
duān

_____

7. 昨晚上天我都没哪儿去，在家就电视看。

_____

8. 那好件衣又看服又便宜。

_____

D Listen to the conversation between 李秋 Lǐ Qiū and 兰兰 Lánlan; then answer the following questions.

1. What did 兰兰 Lánlan plan to do for the weekend? Did she change her mind after this conversation?

2. What did 李秋 Lǐ Qiū plan to do for the weekend?

3. What was 李秋 Lǐ Qiū's mother going to make and why?

4. Could 兰兰 Lánlan and 李秋 Lǐ Qiū make them too?

In the box below, paste the copy of the conversation given to you by your teacher to further check your understanding. Use this copy to hold a conversation with your partner.

E Read the story about 林汉理, then answer the questions.

林汉理一家人来澳大利亚时，林汉理才九岁。他们已经来了六年了，林汉理还没回去过。

这次暑假，林汉理回去北京玩了两个星期。他住叔叔家。叔叔看到他很高兴，说他长得和爸爸很像，只是比爸爸高多了。这次回去，他也看到了很多以前的朋友。他和他们一起踢足球，打网球，听摇滚乐，看电影和逛街，玩得非常高兴。可是，最后两天林汉理感冒了。他发高烧，打喷嚏，又咳嗽，两天都没出去玩儿。叔叔还带他去看了医生。

在回澳大利亚的飞机上，林汉理还咳嗽，也吐了。回到家里，他又睡了两天。不过，林汉理还是觉得这次旅行是最过瘾的一次旅行。

1. Where is 林汉理 from and when did he come here?

2. How did he enjoy his trip back to his home town?

3. How was he received by his relatives there?

4. What happened at the end of his trip?

Writing exercise

How to write a character correctly:

1. Write the strokes according to the numbered sequence.
2. Start each stroke beginning where the number is located.
3. End a stroke with the pen lifted off the paper if it has a pointy end, or with the pen stopped on the paper if it has a round end.

Trace the two lightly printed examples and maintain the proportions in the practice boxes.
The first space is for you to write the Pinyin and meaning of each character.

1

第 | Pinyin: / Meaning: | 第 | 第
课 | P: / M: | 课 | 课
校 | P: / M: | 校 | 校
历 | P: / M: | 历 | 历
史 | P: / M: | 史 | 史
地 | P: / M: | 地 | 地
理 | P: / M: | 理 | 理

	P: M:								
数	数 数								

	P: M:								
科	科 科								

	P: M:								
英	英 英								

	P: M:								
语	语 语								

	P: M:								
美	美 美								

	P: M:								
术	术 术								

	P: M:								
考	考 考								

	P: M:								
试	试 试								

	P: M:								
汉	汉 汉								

	P: M:								
用	用 用								
忘	P: M:								
	忘 忘								
班	P: M:								
	班 班								
教	P: M:								
	教 教								
室	P: M:								
	室 室								
楼	P: M:								
	楼 楼								
新	P: M:								
	新 新								
作	P: M:								
	作 作								
业	P: M:								
	业 业								

2

		P: M:										
路		路	路									
离		P: M:										
		离	离									
远		P: M:										
		远	远									
近		P: M:										
		近	近									
公		P: M:										
		公	公									
骑		P: M:										
		骑	骑									
自		P: M:										
		自	自									
车		P: M:										
		车	车									
从		P: M:										
		从	从									

	P: M:									
长	长	长								

	P: M:									
钟	钟	钟								

	P: M:									
坐	坐	坐								

	P: M:									
汽	汽	汽								

	P: M:									
知	知	知								

	P: M:									
道	道	道								

	P: M:									
门	门	门								

	P: M:									
站	站	站								

	P: M:									
往	往	往								

九十六

过

火

东

南

西

千

百

又

视

3

| P:
M: | | | | | | | | | |
| 过 | 过 | | | | | | | | |

| P:
M: | | | | | | | | | |
| 火 | 火 | | | | | | | | |

| P:
M: | | | | | | | | | |
| 东 | 东 | | | | | | | | |

| P:
M: | | | | | | | | | |
| 南 | 南 | | | | | | | | |

| P:
M: | | | | | | | | | |
| 西 | 西 | | | | | | | | |

| P:
M: | | | | | | | | | |
| 千 | 千 | | | | | | | | |

| P:
M: | | | | | | | | | |
| 百 | 百 | | | | | | | | |

| P:
M: | | | | | | | | | |
| 又 | 又 | | | | | | | | |

| P:
M: | | | | | | | | | |
| 视 | 视 | | | | | | | | |

	P: M:								
节	节	节							

	P: M:								
目	目	目							

	P: M:								
片	片	片							

	P: M:								
听	听	听							

	P: M:								
每	每	每							

	P: M:								
就	就	就							

	P: M:								
影	影	影							

	P: M:								
迷	迷	迷							

	P: M:								
张	张	张							

九十八

		P: M:									
票		票	票								
音		P: M:									
		音	音								
乐		P: M:									
		乐	乐								
歌		P: M:									
		歌	歌								
剧		P: M:									
		剧	剧								
篮		P: M:									
		篮	篮								
足		P: M:									
		足	足								
排		P: M:									
		排	排								
网		P: M:									
		网	网								

	P: M:										
赛	赛 赛										
	P: M:										
贵	贵 贵										
	P: M:										
便	便 便										
	P: M:										
宜	宜 宜										
	P: M:										
唱	唱 唱										
	P: M:										
寿	寿 寿										
	P: M:										
址	址 址										
	P: M:										
街	街 街										
	P: M:										
能	能 能										

5

姨	P: M:								
	姨 姨								
台	P: M:								
	台 台								
祝	P: M:								
	祝 祝								
快	P: M:								
	快 快								
送	P: M:								
	送 送								
久	P: M:								
	久 久								
已	P: M:								
	已 已								
经	P: M:								
	经 经								
己	P: M:								
	己 己								

	P: M:									
像	像 像									
矮	P: M:									
	矮 矮									
短	P: M:									
	短 短									
比	P: M:									
	比 比									
较	P: M:									
	较 较									
包	P: M:									
	包 包									
粽	P: M:									
	粽 粽									
饼	P: M:									
	饼 饼									
糕	P: M:									
	糕 糕									

一〇二

6

		P: M:										
饺		饺	饺									
拿		P: M:										
		拿	拿									
手		P: M:										
		手	手									
病		P: M:										
		病	病									
舒		P: M:										
		舒	舒									
头		P: M:										
		头	头									
疼		P: M:										
		疼	疼									
吐		P: M:										
		吐	吐									
发		P: M:										
		发	发									

	P: M:								
烧	烧 烧								
	P: M:								
肚	肚 肚								
	P: M:								
厕	厕 厕								
	P: M:								
拉	拉 拉								
	P: M:								
带	带 带								
	P: M:								
医	医 医								
	P: M:								
次	次 次								
	P: M:								
感	感 感								
	P: M:								
冒	冒 冒								

开	P: M:								
开 开								
坏	P: M:								
坏 坏								
药	P: M:								
药 药								
休	P: M:								
休 休								
息	P: M:								
息 息								
水	P: M:								
水 水								
假	P: M:								
假 假								
条	P: M:								
条 条								
让	P: M:								
让 让								

7

牙	P: M:									
	牙	牙								

旅	P: M:									
	旅	旅								

暑	P: M:									
	暑	暑								

算	P: M:									
	算	算								

些	P: M:									
	些	些								

方	P: M:									
	方	方								

香	P: M:									
	香	香								

港	P: M:									
	港	港								

金	P: M:									
	金	金								

海	P: M:								
	海	海							
岸	P: M:								
	岸	岸							
机	P: M:								
	机	机							
办	P: M:								
	办	办							
照	P: M:								
	照	照							
相	P: M:								
	相	相							
觉	P: M:								
	觉	觉							
胖	P: M:								
	胖	胖							
凶	P: M:								
	凶	凶							

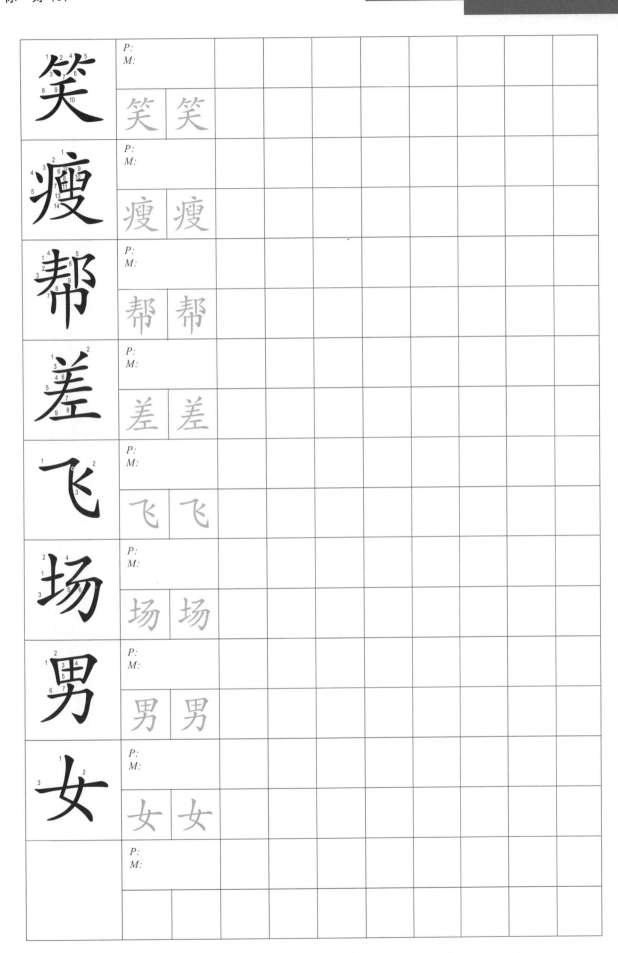

一〇八

	P: M:								
	P: M:								
	P: M:								
	P: M:								
	P: M:								
	P: M:								
	P: M:								
	P: M:								
	P: M:								